Dear Student,

this book will help you to get more out of your music lessons. Your teacher can use it to note down everything you need to work on at home and with enough pages for over 70 lessons it should last you for a well over a year.

There are a few pages of blank manuscript paper at the back of the book so that you can make a note of any tunes, scales or key signatures you need to remember and also a small guide to music theory, in case you forget any of the basics.

If you are preparing for an exam you can use the scale chart to keep track of the scales and arpeggios you are learning.

Good luck with your music practice, and don't forget to take this book with you to every lesson!

Lesson date:

Scales and exercises:

Pieces:

Other work:

This week's tip: *try to practise a little every day.*

Lesson date:

Scales and exercises:

Pieces:

Other work:

This week's tip: *practise slowly before you try to play quickly.*

Lesson date:

Scales and exercises:

Pieces:

Other work:

This week's tip: *practise the difficult bars in the music more than the rest.*

Lesson date:

Scales and exercises:

Pieces:

Other work:

This week's tip: *count out difficult bars and clap the rhythm before you play.*

Lesson date:

Scales and exercises:

Pieces:

Other work:

This week's tip: *if you find reading the notes difficult, try to name them before playing them.*

Lesson date:

Scales and exercises:

Pieces:

Other work:

This week's tip: *if there are words, sing the tune before you play it.*

Lesson date

Scales and exercises:

Pieces:

Other work:

This week's tip: *if there are no words, make some up, then sing the song!*

Lesson date

Scales and exercises:

Pieces:

Other work:

This week's tip: *check that you are using the correct fingering for every note.*

Lesson date

Scales and exercises:

Pieces:

Other work:

This week's tip: *be careful to play the correct rhythms.*

Lesson date

Scales and exercises:

Pieces:

Other work:

This week's tip: *read the music carefully and check you are playing loud and quiet at the correct places.*

Lesson date

Scales and exercises:

Pieces:

Other work:

This week's tip: *check your posture.*

Lesson date

Scales and exercises:

Pieces:

Other work:

This week's tip: *if you can play a piece well, why not play it to family and/or friends?*

Lesson date

Scales and exercises:

Pieces:

Other work:

This week's tip: *aim to sight read at least one piece each week.*

Lesson date

Scales and exercises:

Pieces:

Other work:

This week's tip: *sometimes, when you play through a piece or a scale, give yourself a mark out of 10!*

Lesson date

Scales and exercises:

Pieces:

Other work:

This week's tip: *try to memorise the difficult bits of the music.*

Lesson date

Scales and exercises:

Pieces:

Other work:

This week's tip: *when practising scales, arpeggios or broken chords, make sure that they are at the same speed throughout.*

Lesson date

Scales and exercises:

Pieces:

Other work:

This week's tip: *learn what a chromatic scale is and how to play it.*

Lesson date

Scales and exercises:

Pieces:

Other work:

This week's tip: *sometimes play everything as quietly as you can.*

Lesson date

Scales and exercises:

Pieces:

Other work:

This week's tip: *sometimes play everything as loud as you can.*

Lesson date

Scales and exercises:

Pieces:

Other work:

This week's tip: *if you find it difficult to find time to do enough practice, make sure that you at least do some on the day before your lesson.*

Lesson date

Scales and exercises:

Pieces:

Other work:

This week's tip: *the golden rule with sight reading is "play slowly but keep going".*

Lesson date

Scales and exercises:

Pieces:

Other work:

This week's tip: *when you are sight reading, don't forget to check the key signature.*

Lesson date

Scales and exercises:

Pieces:

Other work:

This week's tip: *start your practice with scales or technical exercises to warm up your fingers (and lips, if you play a wind instrument).*

Lesson date

Scales and exercises:

Pieces:

Other work:

This week's tip: *find a piece you learnt previously and play it again.*

Lesson date

Scales and exercises:

Pieces:

Other work:

This week's tip: *practise the first four bars of your piece more than the rest: you want to make a good start.*

Lesson date

Scales and exercises:

Pieces:

Other work:

This week's tip: *if you can play your scales well, start to play them faster.*

Lesson date

Scales and exercises:

Pieces:

Other work:

This week's tip: *pay special attention to the last few bars of your pieces, you want to finish well and leave a good impression!*

Lesson date

Scales and exercises:

Pieces:

Other work:

This week's tip: *think of a piece of music you like and know well and try to play it by ear.*

Lesson date

Scales and exercises:

Pieces:

Other work:

This week's tip: *once you can play a piece fairly well, try to make up an alternative ending for it.*

Lesson date

Scales and exercises:

Pieces:

Other work:

This week's tip: *can you compose a short introduction to your favourite piece?*

Lesson date

Scales and exercises:

Pieces:

Other work:

This week's tip: *ask your teacher to play to you one of his or her own favourite pieces.*

Lesson date

Scales and exercises:

Pieces:

Other work:

This week's tip: *sometimes play your scales staccato.*

Lesson date

Scales and exercises:

Pieces:

Other work:

This week's tip: *memorise the italian terms at the back of this book!*

Lesson date

Scales and exercises:

Pieces:

Other work:

This week's tip: *tell your teacher what you practised most so that he or she knows to listen to that during your lesson.*

Lesson date

Scales and exercises:

Pieces:

Other work:

This week's tip: *watch someone playing your instrument on youtube.*

Lesson date

Scales and exercises:

Pieces:

Other work:

This week's tip: *sometimes practise your scales and arpeggios with the metronome and check that you are at the correct speed for your grade.*

Lesson date

Scales and exercises:

Pieces:

Other work:

This week's tip: *if possible, join a band, orchestra or choir at your school or in your local area.*

Lesson date

Scales and exercises:

Pieces:

Other work:

This week's tip: *watch a musical (for example The Sound of Music) and learn some of the songs from it.*

Lesson date

Scales and exercises:

Pieces:

Other work:

This week's tip: *if you have a smart phone, ask your teacher if you can record him or her playing one of the pieces you are learning.*

Lesson date

Scales and exercises:

Pieces:

Other work:

This week's tip: *ask your teacher if you can have a go at some duets (either with your teacher or with a friend).*

Lesson date

Scales and exercises:

Pieces:

Other work:

This week's tip: *at Christmas think about performing some carols in aid of charity.*

Lesson date

Scales and exercises:

Pieces:

Other work:

This week's tip: *if your have a smart phone, record yourself playing one of your pieces.*

Lesson date

Scales and exercises:

Pieces:

Other work:

This week's tip: *sometimes get out some really easy music and play through it just for fun.*

Lesson date

Scales and exercises:

Pieces:

Other work:

This week's tip: *if you play the piano, guitar or violin, make sure your finger nails are short enough.*

Lesson date

Scales and exercises:

Pieces:

Other work:

This week's tip: *make sure you are doing enough practice to make progress with the pieces you are practising.*

Lesson date

Scales and exercises:

Pieces:

Other work:

This week's tip: *if you have difficulty in remembering to practise, why not set an alarm on your phone to remind yourself to do it?*

Lesson date

Scales and exercises:

Pieces:

Other work:

This week's tip: *practise drawing some treble and bass clefs on the staves above.*

Lesson date

Scales and exercises:

Pieces:

Other work:

This week's tip: *try to compose a short piece which you can use as a warm up exercise when you practise.*

Lesson date

Scales and exercises:

Pieces:

Other work:

This week's tip: *if it rains this week, cheer yourself up by playing some of your favourite music!*

Lesson date

Scales and exercises:

Pieces:

Other work:

This week's tip: *take a request from a friend. Ask them what music they really like and learn to play it for them.*

Lesson date

Scales and exercises:

Pieces:

Other work:

This week's tip: *make a list of your 10 favourite pieces of music. (Think of pop songs, films, Christmas carols, musicals etc)*

Lesson date

Scales and exercises:

Pieces:

Other work:

This week's tip: *on the above staves, draw the key signature for the key of D major (hint - look in the back of this book).*

Lesson date

Scales and exercises:

Pieces:

Other work:

This week's tip: *teach yourself to whistle and then whistle "Happy Birthday to You".*

Lesson date

Scales and exercises:

Pieces:

Other work:

This week's tip: *work out how many tunes you have learnt to play since you started and write the number here:_____ (You may have to guess!)*

Lesson date

Scales and exercises:

Pieces:

Other work:

This week's tip: *listen to some music by Beethoven. Afterwards give it a mark out of 10 (for how much you liked it).*

Lesson date

Scales and exercises:

Pieces:

Other work:

This week's tip: *listen to some music by Mozart. Afterwards give it a mark out of 10 (for how much you liked it).*

Lesson date

Scales and exercises:

Pieces:

Other work:

This week's tip: *listen to some music by Tchiakovsky. Afterwards give it a mark out of 10 (for how much you liked it).*

Lesson date

Scales and exercises:

Pieces:

Other work:

This week's tip: *what is the highest note you can play on your instrument? Ask your teacher to write it on the stave above.*

Lesson date

Scales and exercises:

Pieces:

Other work:

This week's tip: *what is the lowest note you can play on your instrument? Ask your teacher to write it on the stave above.*

Lesson date

Scales and exercises:

Pieces:

Other work:

This week's tip: *on the stave above, write the key signature for the key of F major.*

Lesson date

Scales and exercises:

Pieces:

Other work:

This week's tip: *on the stave above, write 3 bars of music in triple time.*

Lesson date

Scales and exercises:

Pieces:

Other work:

This week's tip: *on the staves above, copy out the first 2 bars of one of the pieces you are now learning.*

Lesson date

Scales and exercises:

Pieces:

Other work:

This week's tip: *learn how to play "Happy Birthday to You" so that you can play it for your family or friends on their birthdays.*

Lesson date

Scales and exercises:

Pieces:

Other work:

This week's tip: *if it is nearly Christmas, ask your teacher if you can play some Christmas carols.*

Lesson date

Scales and exercises:

Pieces:

Other work:

This week's tip: *learn how to play the National Anthem.*

Lesson date

Scales and exercises:

Pieces:

Other work:

This week's tip: *write some rests on the staves above.* *1) a quaver 2) a crotchet 3) a minim 4) a semibreve*

Lesson date

Scales and exercises:

Pieces:

Other work:

This week's tip: *on the staves above, write the key signature for the key of D minor.*

Lesson date

Scales and exercises:

Pieces:

Other work:

This week's tip: *play this clapping game. Ask your teacher to clap a tune and you try and guess what it is. Then do it the other way around.*

Lesson date

Scales and exercises:

Pieces:

Other work:

This week's tip: *don't forget the dynamics. Remember, forte (f) means loud, piano(p) means quiet and crescendo means gradually get louder.*

Lesson date

Scales and exercises:

Pieces:

Other work:

This week's tip: *listen to some music on the radio and write down what you heard here:*_____

Lesson date

Scales and exercises:

Pieces:

Other work:

This week's tip: *ask your teacher if you can learn to play a duet with a friend.*

Lesson date

Scales and exercises:

Pieces:

Other work:

This week's tip: *ask your teacher if you can learn to play a trio with two other friends.*

Lesson date

Scales and exercises:

Pieces:

Other work:

This week's tip: *keep practising ....never give up!*

Basic Music Theory

 This is a treble clef.

𝄢: This is a bass clef.

In piano music the right hand plays the treble clef notes.

In piano music the left hand plays the bass clef notes.

Note values:

𝅝 = semibreve - 4 beats

𝅗𝅥 = minim - 2 beats

𝅘𝅥 = crotchet -1 beat

𝅘𝅥𝅮 = quaver - ½ beat

𝅘𝅥𝅯 = semiquaver - ¼ beat

Time signatures:

Simple time:

$\frac{2}{4}$ two crotchet beats per bar

$\frac{3}{4}$ three crotchet beats per bar

$\frac{4}{4}$ four crotchet beats per bar

Compound time:

$\frac{6}{8}$ two dotted crotchet beats per bar

$\frac{9}{8}$ three dotted crotchet beats per bar

$\frac{12}{8}$ four dotted crotchet beats per bar

Common Italian terms:

p *(piano)* = quiet

f *(forte)* = loud

mp *(mezzo piano)* = moderately quiet

mf *(mezzo forte)* = moderately loud

pp *(pianissimo)* = very quiet

ff *(fortissimo)* = very loud

cresc. = gradually get louder

dim. = gradually get quieter

allegro = quick

andante = at a medium speed

lento = slow

presto = very fast

Note names:

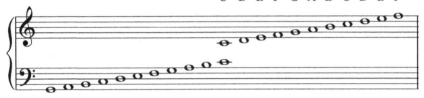

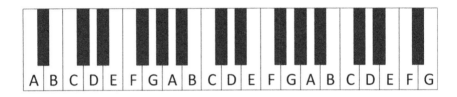

Accidentals:

♯ = a sharp, raises the note that follows by a semitone

♭ = a flat, lowers the note that follows by a semitone

♮ = a natural, cancels a sharp or flat

Key signatures:

C major	G major	D major	F major	B♭ major
and	and	and	and	and
A minor	E minor	B minor	D minor	G minor

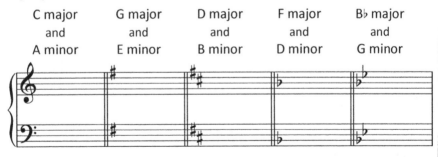

Scale Chart

This list shows most of the common scales and arpeggios that you need to know in the early grades. Tick the box once you know a scale or arpeggio so that you can keep track of what you have done.

	Scale	Arpeggio
C major		
G major		
D major		
A major		
E major		
B major		
F major		
B♭ major		
E♭ major		
A♭ major		
A minor		
E minor		
B minor		
F♯ minor		
C♯ minor		
D minor		
G minor		
C minor		
F minor		

More books for young pianists

Young pianists will love these exciting books which have been designed to make practice fun and easy!

PIANO SCALES GRADE 1 - WITH PICTURES

Kids often struggle to remember the notes and fingering for scales and standard musical notation doesn't help much.

This striking book encourages practice. Large print and lots of colourful pictures make this the easiest way to learn all of the scales and broken chords set for grade 1 piano. This book is suitable for even the youngest pianist.

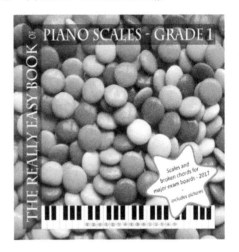

PIANO GRADE 1 IN EASY STEPS

Pianists who want to take grade 1 but need to approach it in easy steps can try these pre grade 1 books. They each contain a selection of all of the types of test which are found in a real grade 1 exam:

       9 pieces (the student chooses 3 to learn)

       Scales and broken chords

       Aural tests

       Theory

       Mark sheet and certificate

MUSIC MANUSCRIPT BOOK

Kids love learning to draw treble and bass clefs and can take their first steps in music composition with this fun little manuscript book.
Six large staves on each page make this super easy for littlies to use.

Music Manuscript Book
36 pages - 6 large staves per page

SMOKE SIGNALS

Get those feet tapping with these rhythmic and tuneful pieces!
Kids love to play music which has a strong beat with repeating patterns

SMOKE SIGNALS
Easy piano tunes in an American Indian style

Grade 1 piano

and, guess what, music like this is easy to play.
This fun book has 12 American Indian style pieces, all easy, and each piece comes with a colourful illustration and interesting preparatory exercises. Bite sized facts about the history of the American Indians will help to kick start the imagination of children and make practice more fun.
The tunes are suitable for kids from age 7 and up and progress in standard from very easy to about grade 1.

Made in the USA
Monee, IL
10 December 2023

48400153R00046